T0346968

A POSTCARD
FROM THE
WYE

JAN DOBRZYNSKI & KEITH TURNER

First published in 2008
Reprinted 2014

The History Press
The Mill, Brimscombe Port,
Stroud, Gloucestershire, GL5 2QG
www.thehistorypress.co.uk

British Library Cataloguing in Publication Data
A catalogue record for this book is available from the British Library.

ISBN 978-0-7509-4850-0

Typeset in 10.5/13.5pt Photina.
Typesetting and origination by
The History Press.
Printed and bound in Great Britain by
Marston Book Services Limited, Oxfordshire

Contents

Introduction   5

1.   To Rhayader & the Reservoirs   7

2.   Through the Heart of Wales   33

3.   A Very English River   47

4.   The Romantic Wye   67

5.   The Monmouthshire Wye   105

The course of the River Wye.

The Wye takes it's rise near the summit of Plinlimon; and dividing the counties of Radnor and Brecknoc, passes through the middle of Herefordshire. From thence becoming a second boundary between Monmouth, and Glocestershire, it falls into the Severn, a little below Chepstow. To this place from Ross, which is a course of near forty miles, it flows in a gentle, uninterrupted stream; and adorns, through it's various reaches, a succession of the most picturesque scenes.

(William Gilpin, *Observations on the River Wye*, 1770)

Introduction

Flowing some 135 miles from the slopes of Plynlimon near Cardigan Bay to the Bristol Channel, the Wye is the second longest of the great rivers of Wales, and one of the most delightful in Britain. Known to the Welsh as Afon Gwy, the Wye has for centuries been a source of food and employment, a boundary, a trade route, a place of leisure and quiet enjoyment, a haven for wildlife, an inspiration for artists and writers – and the birthplace of the very idea of tourism in Britain.

It is in the nature of things that a river as long as the Wye, during its journey to the sea, will undergo a number of significant transformations. To begin with, the initial trickle from its source in bog or spring will, as it gathers pace, quickly become a fast-flowing stream, though narrow enough to be crossed in one bound. Soon, though, it widens as it gathers more water from its valley and presents rather more of an obstacle, and that single leap has to be replaced by a succession of jumps from one stepping stone to another. Simple bridges now appear and, as the river broadens further, fording points are established where its bed is hard enough, and its level low enough, to allow the safe passage of foot-travellers, livestock and vehicles.

The river then enters its middle age, occupying the valley it has carved for itself from the surrounding landscape over countless millennia. Swelled by a myriad of tributary ditches and streams, it is now deep enough to carry commercial vessels. Passing the upper limit of navigation it becomes a trading highway lined with quays and warehouses; gone are the fords and simple one-arched bridges, replaced by ferries and spans high enough not to hinder the passage of the all-important boats beneath. Finally, the river enters its old age as it nears the sea or, in the case of the Wye, a greater river. Now tidal in nature, it passes its lowest bridging point before merging seamlessly with an ever-widening expanse of water.

The story of the Wye begins in a peat bog between the twin peaks of Pumlumon Fawr (2,468ft) and Arwystli (2,427ft) on the eastern slopes of the mountainous dome of Pumlomon – Plynlimon in English – a little to the east of Aberystwyth in the old county of Montgomeryshire (now part of Powys). Just under 2 miles to the north, the Afon Hafren (the River Severn), also rises, destined – somewhat astonishingly – to join the Wye at the end of both rivers' journeys. Whereas the Severn takes a very circuitous route to the Bristol Channel, the Wye does not, flowing as it does in a much more direct line, thus accounting for the difference of nearly 90 miles between their two lengths. From Plynlimon, the mountain stream that is the young Afon Gwy begins its generally south-easterly journey through farmland and forest, rocky gorges and rapids. Shortly after leaving the desolate slopes of the mountain it is joined by the A44 from Aberystwyth, which it parallels to the small town of Llangurig – indeed, from here on to its confluence with the

Severn the river will be closely paralleled for virtually its entire length by either road or railway (and sometimes both), the builders of these other two great trading highways taking advantage of the comparatively level valley floor so thoughtfully smoothed out for them by the river.

Continuing south-eastwards through Powys, the Afon Gwy crosses the old Radnorshire border and, passing the market town of Rhayader, then delineates the former boundary of Radnor with Brecknockshire. The river leaves the land of its birth behind when, in the first major deviation from its south-easterly course, it swings north-eastwards just before Hay-on-Wye to cross into Herefordshire; as the town's name proclaims, at this point it assumes the title of the Wye. Meandering eastwards through the lush, cattle-fattening country of the Marches, it reaches the city of Hereford – the only city on the river – before wandering south through Ross-on-Wye and, after briefly skirting Gloucestershire, crosses into that not-quite-Welsh, not-quite-English county of Monmouthshire.

This final reach of the Wye is perhaps its section of greatest historical importance: through the beautiful gorge of Symonds Yat, across the border to Monmouth and on past the picturesque ruins of Tintern Abbey. The word 'picturesque' is used advisedly for the possession of 'Picturesque Beauty' was the key criterion, advanced by William Gilpin in his *Observations on the River Wye* of 1770, for determining whether or not a place was worth visiting. This was a new and alien concept for British travellers and tourists, who had hitherto dismissed the uncultivated landscape as seriously unpleasant, frightful and gloomy. Gilpin's best-selling volume – the first in a series – set tourism on a completely new course, with the new, Romantic movement in the arts a direct consequence of it as writers and painters endeavoured to capture in words and pictures the untamed nature of the wilder regions of the British Isles.

And so to Chepstow and the Wye's rendezvous with the Severn, which it joins in a confluence of waters half a mile wide. Downstream is the Bristol Channel and, beyond that, the open sea.

Just as the Severn has its own long-distance footpath from source to estuary, the Severn Way opened in 1997, so the Wye has a similar uninterrupted, way-marked walking trail beside the river. Linking with a number of local and regional paths, the Wye Valley Walk (or Llwybr Dyffryn Gwy), opened fully in 2002, runs for 136 miles from Hafren Forest and the source of the river to the Severn at Chepstow (though its official orientation is from mouth to source).

Finally, a word of warning to other postcard collectors. There is a much shorter River Wye, a tributary of the Derwent, in Derbyshire, and an even shorter one, a tributary of the Thames, in Buckinghamshire; occasionally it is difficult, without recourse to a detailed gazetteer, to tell which river a particular card is from.

Details of the course of each section of the Wye Valley Walk, in relation to the river, can be found at the beginning of each chapter, and between captions. All the postcards included in this book are from the authors' collections. Publication details are given at the end of the captions, if and as they appear on the cards.

1

To Rhayader & the Reservoirs

For nine miles the stream dashes through wild and rugged country,
through moorland and bog, and then runs by the side of the road to
Llangerig, below which village opens the first of the numerous
picturesque views presented in the Valley of the Wye.
  (*The Wye Valley. From Plynlimon to Hereford*, Great Western Railway, 1923)

The Wye Valley Walk actually begins in Ryd-y-benwch car park near the start of
the Severn Way. From there it follows that path back past the source of the Severn
to the source of the Wye, some 2 miles distant, then follows that river southwards
fairly closely all the way to Llangurig.

A multi-view postcard showing views of the Wye Valley. (*Unidentified*)

211137 J.V. Source of the River Wye, Plynlimon Pass

Where the 135-mile journey begins: the boggy source of the River Wye, or Afon Gwy, roughly 2,400ft above sea level high on the slopes of Plynlimon. (*Valentine's*)

The uppermost reach of the Afon Gwy displays all the characteristics of a young mountain stream: a rocky bed, shallow water and an often precipitous, winding course through desolate, treeless moorland. Eisteddfa Gurig means 'rest place of Curig' (see p. 11), Curig being the sixth-century Irish monk associated with the region and who is reputed to have sheltered here – though exactly how would seem uncertain, given the nature of the landscape. (*Galloway, Aberystwyth*)

Another card from the same local publisher, showing the young river threading its way south-eastwards through Plynlimon Pass towards its rendezvous with its first tributary the Afon Tarrenig, the A44 and the village of Llangurig. (*Galloway, Aberystwyth*)

A third Galloway card of the Wye close to its source. The fact that the postcard's own caption gives the river its English, rather than Welsh, name suggests that it was intended for sale to tourists from over the border. (*Galloway, Aberystwyth*)

Some 2 miles from its source the Afon Gwy reaches the A44, which it will follow closely all the way to Rhayader. Here the valley – like its river – deepens and broadens, and shows the first signs of a human presence. (*E.T.W. Dennis & Sons, Ltd. London & Scarborough*)

The first village on the Afon Gwy is Llangurig, named after the sixth-century monastic settlement founded here by St Curig (who died in 550). The present-day church is late medieval, rebuilt in 1879 by George Gilbert Scott, better known as the architect of St Pancras station in London. Llangurig was formerly a staging post for changing coach horses before crossing Plynlimon to the coast and its 'highest village in Wales' claim to fame is based on its situation 1,045ft above sea level. (*Unidentified*)

Below Llangurig the Wye Valley Walk strays westwards from the river for 4 miles or so, crossing into the neighbouring valley of the River Dernol.

About 2½ miles before Rhayader the Gwy is joined from the east by the Afon Marteg; immediately before they merge the tributary is crossed by Marteg Bridge (Pont Marteg) carrying the A470. The view here, probably captured in the 1930s, is looking north back up the valley of the Wye; the wooden footbridge allowed the tenants on the Dderw estate to reach the road and was replaced by a steel one in 1979 by Bernard Lloyd of Rhayader, for the local angling society. It was here that the former Mid-Wales Railway crossed from the Marteg valley to the Wye valley on its way from Llanidloes on the Cambrian Railways line to Aberystwyth. (*Salmon Series, J. Salmon Ltd., Sevenoaks*)

Little has changed in this postcard view which was sent in 1961: the stone wall by the bridge has been mended, the road has a centre line and a handful of vehicles now intrude to disturb the tranquillity of the valley, including a motorcycle and sidecar combination, and an ancient-looking caravan; the caravanner is talking to someone from a vehicle on the road to St Harmon who has returned to close the gate guarding the road. The photograph was clearly taken and the card first issued long before it was bought and sent – keeping the same cards in print for many years has always been a common practice of postcard publishers. (*Valentine's*)

The Marteg Falls above the confluence of the two rivers. Then as now the spectacle is at its best after a period of heavy rainfall on the high moorland of the river's catchment area. (*WHS Kingsway Real Photo Series*)

The Wye Valley Walk, now back with the Wye, crosses the river on the footbridge and follows the railway formation up the Marteg valley, diverging at a sealed tunnel entrance, as far as the visitor centre at Gilfach, a 4,000-year-old megalithic site. It then heads south again, across country to Rhayader.

Approaching Rhayader, the first town on the Wye. This scene is just below Pont Marteg, with the road and the reinforced railway embankment above it heading southward. (*J. Salmon Ltd., Sevenoaks*)

Before Rhayader is reached the river is crossed by another footbridge (one of several such private structures on this stretch of the river), this one built in 1930 by Morgan Lloyd & Sons of Rhayader to enable tenants of the Gwardolau estate to reach the main road. Constructed with a wooden deck on iron beams, it was damaged beyond repair in the winter floods of 1960/1 and never repaired. This card was posted in 1948, the photograph being taken roughly at the middle point of the bridge's life. (*Valentine's 'Bromotype' Series*)

A Rhayader multi-view card, depicting scenes from the neighbouring reservoirs. This type of card was popular with tourists, either to send or keep as a souvenir, as it delivered more pictures for the price of a conventional postcard. Today the town is a centre for holiday and leisure activities such as pony trekking, fishing and walking. (*Frith's Series, F. Frith & Co., Ltd., Reigate*)

The church of St Winifred, built in 1778 and completely rebuilt in 1866, serving the community of Llansantffraed Cwmdeuddwr on the western bank of the Wye from Rhayader. (*Photochrom Co. Ltd. London & Tunbridge Wells*)

The market town of Rhayader derives its English name from the Welsh Rhaeadr Gwy, 'the waterfall on the Gwy'. The town bridge was built over the waterfall, partly destroying it, leaving a series of rapids (through still very impressive when the river is high). Just below the bridge the Bwgey brook trickles into the river; this once ran down North Street and West Street, with stone slabs over it allowing pedestrians to cross, but was fully buried in 1877. Local tradition has it that anyone stepping into the brook will return to Rhayader. (*Unidentified*)

The old bridge at Rhayader was built in 1780 to carry the mountain coach road to Devil's Bridge and Aberystwyth, and later connected the town with its railway station across the river. In 1929 Radnorshire County Council strengthened it with concrete, the result being that its distinctive hump was flattened out, as is apparent here. The road over it is now designated the B4518 and is used by the thousands of tourists visiting the Elan Valley each year. (*Valentine's 'Bromotype' Series*)

West Street joined onto Bridge Street to cross the river and was also part of the mountain coach road, which accounts for it being flanked by inns and hostelries as befits a major coaching centre and many have survived to this day. The town's market building (centre) has however not survived, for it was demolished in the 1920s to ease congestion at the crossroads here and a war memorial and clock tower erected in its place. (*Valentine's Series*)

Rhayader station was opened on 21 September 1864 by the Mid Wales Railway (later taken over by the Cambrian Railways and then the Great Western), and was closed on the last day of December 1962 by British Railways. The long, north–south line through the heart of Wales on which it stood provided a connecting link between the Shrewsbury–Aberystwyth route in mid-Wales, via Caersws, and the South Wales network, via Builth Wells. (*J. Roberts, Chemist, Rhayader*)

Rhayader has four main streets named after the four main points of the compass; the clock tower stands at the centre of the town's resulting cruciform layout. This view is from East Street . . . (*Valentine's 'Bromotype' Series*)

. . . while this post-Second World War one is from West Street. The town's distinctive but simple street pattern arose from the fact that four major turnpike roads met here: from north and south in the Wye Valley, west from the Elan Valley and east from Presteigne and the borders. The area was also criss-crossed with ancient drovers' routes to Hereford, Gloucester and London. (*Valentine's*)

CITY OF BIRMINGHAM WATER DEPARTMENT.

VISIT OF THEIR MAJESTIES

THE KING AND QUEEN

TO

THE ELAN VALLEY WORKS, RHAYADER,

AND

OPENING OF THE NEW SUPPLY

BY

HIS MAJESTY THE KING,

JULY 21ST, 1904.

ROYAL PROGRAMME.

HALLEWELL ROGERS,
LORD MAYOR.

The Elan Valley is inseparable from Rhayader, and its massive nineteenth-century reservoirs built to supply Birmingham with clean water are a major tourist attraction in the region. This is the front page of the official programme issued to the VIPs of the day invited to witness the project's royal opening.

The Elan Valley - Arrival of the King and Queen at the new Birmingham Waterworks.

A whole network of railways was laid to facilitate the construction of the reservoirs, and part of the system was used to convey the royal visitors and guests to the opening ceremony, which was held by the filter beds where the water was collected and filtered before it began its long journey to England. The locomotive *Calettwr* sports the royal crest and above it the initials of the Birmingham Corporation Water Works, and has brought the official party on a short inspection tour of the Craig Coch Dam. (*'Scott' Series*)

Birmingham Waterworks, Elan Valley
His Majesty The King
Performing the opening Cermony
July 21. 1904

This historic postcard captures the moment when King Edward VII, accompanied by Queen Alexandra, discharges his official duty. The party has alighted from the royal train at a specially constructed platform by the filter beds. (*The Spa Series, The Landscape Photographic & Fine Art Publishing Co., Llandrindod Wells*)

The westernmost reservoir of the system is the Claerwen Reservoir, added in the 1950s to increase the overall capacity. It is not actually on the Afon Elan but its tributary, the Afon Claerwen, and material for the dam's construction was brought in by road as opposed to rail. (*Judges' Ltd., Hastings*)

Craig Coch Reservoir and its dam (No. 5), looking north; the name means 'red rock' in Welsh. This is the northernmost reservoir of the system, the first to stem the flow of the Elan. (*RA Series, W.G. Bacon, Stationer, Rhayader*)

CRAIG GOCH DAM & RESERVOIR,
ELAN VALLEY, NEAR RHAYADER

At each dam a tablet is fixed giving statistics for that particular dam and reservoir. At Craig Coch they are: Total capacity – 2,000,000,000 gallons; top water area – 217 acres; top water level – 1,040ft above Ordnance Datum; height of dam above river bed – 120ft; estimated quantity of masonry – 90,372 cu yds; depth of foundations below river bed – 17ft; length of weir – 417ft 6in.; width of dam at base – 115ft. These figures are roughly comparable for the other dams in the system and give a good idea of the vast nature of the whole enterprise. (*J. Roberts, Stationer, Rhayader*)

A North Wales Water Dam.

Craig Coch Dam again, this time simply captioned as 'a North Wales dam'. The card was posted in Birmingham though the reservoirs were a great source of pride not only for the citizens of that city but also for the nation as a whole, offering as they did an example of how to provide the growing urban masses with a seemingly limitless supply of uncontaminated water. (*Delittle, Fenwick & Co., York, for Shurey's Publications*)

Craig-Goch Dam, Elan Valley

A closer view of the Craig Coch Dam, its distinctive curvature enhanced dramatically by the overflowing water on its way down to the Pen-y-Garreg Reservoir below. (Valentine's Series)

Looking north towards Pen-y-Garreg Reservoir, with a short stretch of the Elan Valley floor in the foreground left unsubmerged between its dam and the next reservoir. (*Frith's Series, F. Frith & Co., Ltd., Reigate*)

Pen-y-Garreg Dam in 1904 during the final stages of its construction. Note the contractor's crane on its track along the face of the dam, and a contractor's railway line in the foreground running up to the dam wall. (*Valentine's Series*)

Pen-y-Garreg Dam completed, and the reservoir behind full to overflowing, seen from the road running along its south side. (*Unidentified*)

Pen-y-Garreg Dam, in a most unusual view from the centre of the Afon Elan. The minor road bridge is still here, while the building on the left is now a toilet block serving a camp park. (*Unidentified*)

Below Pen-y-Garreg is the Garreg Ddu Reservoir. This view is looking south with, on the left, the B4518 from Rhayader and the trackbed of one of the construction railways. (*Valentine's Series*)

The southern end of the Garreg Ddu Reservoir in its sylvan setting. Immediately below its unusual dam – its crest is 40ft below top water level with an impressive masonry road bridge on top of that – is the western arm of the Caban Coch Reservoir. ('*Collo Colour*' *4049v Style Postcard, Valentine & Sons Ltd., Dundee and London*)

The Garreg Ddu Dam at a time of a much higher water level. The circular structure beyond is the Foel Tower, the take-off point for the reservoir's water. (*Wallace Jones, Builth Wells & Rhayader*)

A similar view of the Garreg Ddu Dam, this time from road level. Possibly the driver of the car has stepped out to take the photograph; his passenger certainly appears uninterested in the surrounding scenery. (*Unidentified*)

The most southern and eastern of the Elan reservoirs is the Caban Coch Reservoir. Here the waters from the three reservoirs to the north, and the Claerwen to the west, are stored before filtration. (*T.C. Price, Chemist, Rhayader*)

The Caban Coch Reservoir again. It is also the lowest and hence most sheltered of them all, and consequently thickly wooded on both sides. (*J. Salmon Ltd., Sevenoaks*)

ELAN VALLEY. *Caban-Coch Dam.*

The Caban Coch Dam soon after completion, with the various buildings associated with the filter beds to the fore. (*Exclusive Grano Series, The Photochrom Co., Ltd., London and Tunbridge Wells*)

The dam again, the overflow in even more dramatic mode. Like the preceding cards, this would have been sold to tourists wishing to impress the recipient with the majesty and force of nature – and how it had been tamed by modern technology, muscle and craft. (*Wallace Jones's Studio, Builth Wells & Rhayader*)

Water from the feed tower at Caban Coch Dam was routed through filter beds cut into the hillside just below it on the northern side of the Elan. Filtration at this end of the supply line was necessary not for health reasons but to prevent any build-up of organic residues in the iron pipes that took the water to Birmingham. (*P.B. Abery, Photographer, Builth Wells*)

The Elan Valley aqueduct passes through five old counties – Radnorshire, Herefordshire, Shropshire, Worcestershire and Staffordshire – on its 73½-mile journey to Frankley Reservoir on the outskirts of Birmingham. The water is not pumped but flows under the influence of gravity, over a drop of some 170ft, at a rate of 75 million gallons a day. Here the pipeline is seen emerging from its normal underground location to cross the Wye's sister river, the Severn, above Bewdley. (*E.P. Shepherd, Bewdley. V.&S. Ltd., D.*)

MILL AND CASTLE HILL, RHAYADER

This view of the Wye, from north-west of Rhayader, was taken from the ditch and earthworks constituting the only tangible remains left of a castle built in about 1178 by a local chieftain, Rhys ap Gruffydd, as a defence against the Normans. A corn mill stands by the river; its leat and the Gwyn Llyn Brook that feeds it both flow under the railway embankment and Rhayader station on their way to join the waters of the Wye. The mill remained in use up to the Second World War. (*Valentine's 'Bromotype' Series*)

Gwyn Llyn (Lake), a popular fishing spot on the Gwyn Llyn Brook a mile or so outside Rhayader, looking north-westwards up the valley. (*Valentine's Series*)

BUILTH ROAD, RHAYADER

Below Rhayader the Gwy continues on its generally southerly course, closely tracked by the A470 on its eastern bank all the way to Builth Wells. This view is from the main road just beyond the town, looking south-west towards the great, largely uninhabited plateau that rises to nearly 2,000ft on the river's western flank. (*Valentine's*)

A rather earlier view from almost the same location, this time looking back north-westwards to Rhayader across the sharp bend in the river below the town. Half a mile or so to the left the waters of the Afon Elan – or what is left of them – help swell the Gwy, now very much a river on its way to maturity. (*E.M. & A.M. Jones, Rhayader, Radnorshire*)

2

Through the Heart of Wales

Here, too, the Wye scenery is full of charm, and of countless beauties.
(*The Wye Valley. From Plynlimon to Hereford*, Great Western Railway, 1923)

The Wye Valley Walk leaves Rhayader via the road bridge and runs south, some way from the river, until it crosses the Elan where it meets the Wye.

A typical greetings postcard from Builth Wells. (*The Spa Series*)

Immediately below the point where the Elan and Wye meet was a location known as Cerrig Gwynion sidings on the former Cambrian Railways line here in the Wye Valley. The sidings, in the right foreground on the eastern bank of the river, were where stone was laden from a local quarry into railway wagons for transporting up to the Elan reservoir construction sites. Note the white gate protecting the sidings. (*Valentine's Series*)

South of the Elan the Wye Valley Walk again detours away from the river before rejoining it at Llanwrthwl.

The next settlement of any size down the river is Llanwrthwl, with its church of St Gwrthwl prominent in this view. There is a 6ft-high standing stone by the church's south porch – evidence of the widespread practice of establishing Christian churches on earlier pagan sites. (*Unidentified*)

A mile or so below Llanwrthwl lies the Doldowlod Estate, situated on the eastern bank below the village of that name. The original farmhouse was acquired by James Watt, the celebrated engineer, and the estate was thereafter enlarged by his son (also James). In all, three private bridges were built across the Wye to serve the estate, this one being the Ystrad suspension bridge, built in about 1880 from components supplied by the Llanidloes Railway Foundry. It was completely restored in 1989 by Hope & Son of Newbridge-on-Wye (the next village down the river) and is now listed as a National Heritage structure. (*Valentine's*)

Shortly after leaving Llanwrthwl the Wye Valley Walk leaves the river again, rejoining it 3 miles above Builth Wells.

The Wye as it enters Builth Wells, at Pen-ddol Rocks, a beauty spot just north of the town. These outcrops in its bed and banks, not yet eroded away, indicate that the river has not yet achieved full maturity. (*F. Frith & Co., Ltd., Reigate*)

Half a mile below Pen-ddol Rocks the Wye is joined, from the south-west, by the Afon Irfon and together the two waterways define the northern and western boundaries of the old town of Builth Wells. (*Unidentified*)

Builth from the Wye

Builth Wells probably originated as a settlement after the construction of its Norman castle on a hill south of the river overlooking a Roman fording point. In 1277 Edward I began its reconstruction as part of his great chain of castles designed to keep the Welsh in order, though only the site remains today. (*Valentine's Series*)

Builth Bridge was built in 1779, by James Parry of Hay, and replaced a succession of frequently damaged wooden structures. It serves to carry the north–south A470 and the east–west A483 as they cross and has been embellished, strengthened and widened over the years to cope with the increasing demands placed upon it, though it still appears very much as it did when constructed. This view is from upstream. (*Valentine's Series*)

Builth Bridge from downstream. The bridge formerly linked Radnorshire on the north bank (right) with Breconshire on the south, both old counties since 1974 being part of Powys. (*Valentine's Series*)

The bridge close to, before its 1925 doubling in width. By this point the river has travelled 50 miles from its source. (*Unidentified*)

Builth has been a spa town since the eighteenth century, the two principal water sources being Park Wells and Glanne Wells, both close to the Irfon – hence the addition of 'Wells' to its original name of Buellt, Buallt, Bealt then finally Builth in the nineteenth century. Here foul-smelling (and foul-tasting!) salt- and sulphur-rich waters would be bathed in, or even drunk, by those in search of 'the cure'. (*Unidentified*)

In 1691, just before Christmas, virtually the whole of Builth was destroyed by fire, the only substantial building to escape being the stone wool market. Monetary relief was sent from all over Britain – an unprecedented occurrence at the time. The town was rebuilt, and prospered, as this busy Edwardian market day scene would appear to indicate. (*J.B. Hinchcliffe, Publisher, Builth Wells*)

Any spa town worth its salt had to provide – and advertise that fact – all manner of amenities in order to attract custom away from its rivals. Builth was fortunate in having on its doorstep a river on which its Victorian and Edwardian visitors could partake of the new craze for genteel boating. (*Valentine's Series*)

Builth Wells, looking westwards from the village of Llanelwedd on the north bank of the Wye. By the latter part of the nineteenth century Builth was booming, its hotels, guest houses and shops patronised by the great numbers of visitors brought in by the railways. Although the spa's importance has greatly diminished, other visitors have been arriving since 1963 when the Royal Welsh Showground was established midway between here and the town. (*Wallace Jones's Studio, Builth Wells & Rhayader*)

At Llyswen the river ceases its more or less constant progress southwards and doubles back on itself before swinging north-eastwards towards Hay-on-Wye and the English border. On the northern bank is the village of Boughrood, which lends its name to the stone bridge carrying the B4350. It was opened as a toll bridge in 1842 though the toll house (now a private residence) was added later. It was widened in 1959. The photographer of this card has captured a moment of extremely low water – note the high arches, wide foreshore, exposed rocks and the cow having a drink in mid-stream. (*Valentine's*)

After Builth Wells the Wye Valley Walk continues southwards, a mile or more from the river, until it reaches Boughrood Bridge where it crosses from the river's south bank to the north, which it then follows more or less closely to Hay-on-Wye.

Glimpsed here is the single-span lattice-girder bridge built by the Mid Wales Railway in 1864 at Llyswen; after the line closed in 1962 the span was removed. The river appears to be in full spate, the date being – according to the hand-written annotation on the back – May 1920. (*Unidentified*)

Hay-on-Wye is a marcher town, just inside Wales, its Welsh name being Y Gelli ('the grove'). It also straddles the former boundary between Radnorshire and Breconshire. The view is to the south towards the mass of the Black Mountains, rearing to over 2,600ft between here and Abergavenny. (*Raphael Tuck & Sons, Ltd. London*)

The Warren, Hay.

Hay grew as a medieval walled town around its Norman castle – another one strengthened by Edward I – though this had fallen into ruin by the end of the sixteenth century. The Warren, seen here on the right beyond the bend in the river, is a promontory just upstream of the town. The Wye in fact doubles back on itself here to flow between the mass of trees centre right and the buildings of Hay in the distance. (*Unidentified*)

A peaceful scene near Hay on the Wye which, as it prepares to enter Herefordshire, has at last reached maturity. (*Grant, Stationer, Hay*)

Believe it or not, this is the old lattice-girder road bridge across the Wye, built in 1868 by the noted railway contractor Thomas Savin (and raised so high so as to carry the road over the Hereford, Hay & Brecon Railway he was then in the process of constructing). It replaced a much-repaired bridge dating from 1763 and was in turn replaced by a concrete structure in 1957. (*H.R. Grant, Stationer, Hay*)

The tranquil, middle-aged Wye, as seen from the bridge. (*Raphael Tuck & Sons, Ltd*)

At Hay the Wye Valley Walk crosses into the town from the north bank of the river via the new bridge.

Even by accepted standards, Hay Castle has had a very chequered history. Norman in origin, it was burnt by King John in 1216, later razed by Owen Glendower, then partly blown up during the English Civil War. In more modern times it was destroyed by fire again in 1977. Cared for by a charitable trust since 2011, it was formerly owned by Richard Booth, the self-styled 'King of Hay', whose initial 1961 second-hand book business led to Hay becoming the largest second-hand book centre in the world. (*Unidentified*)

The principal thoroughfare in Hay – whose name derives from the Norman French 'haie' meaning hedge or enclosure – is Broad Street, now full of bookshops. The town, as a direct consequence of its international fame as a book centre (and its annual literary festival) also boasts a plethora of fine hotels, restaurants, food and craft shops. (*Frith's Series, Reigate*)

Broad Street on market day in an earlier age. As well as being an important market town, Hay lay on the coach road to Brecon and was therefore well-equipped with pubs and inns, several of which survive today. Other visitors came for sporting reasons, for the sender has written: 'Came here to play cricket against Hay. I got a good score.' (*Raphael Tuck & Sons' 'Framed Aquagraph' Postcard Series, Thomas Moxon, Stationer etc., Castle Street, Hay*)

A pair of tickets from the Hereford, Hay & Brecon Railway's line post-1923 when it was part of the London, Midland & Scottish Railway route from England to the South Wales coalfields, plus a pair of luggage labels relating to the Hereford, Ross & Gloucester Railway issued after its amalgamation with the Great Western.

River Wye and Bridge from Railway Station

Hay railway station, on the southern bank of the Wye, was opened on 11 July 1864 by the Hereford, Hay & Brecon Railway and was closed, as Hay-on-Wye, on 13 June 1955 by British Railways. The view is looking west towards the bridge featured on p. 43. Curiously, the station straddled the English/Welsh border, the eastern end being in Herefordshire and the western in Breconshire!

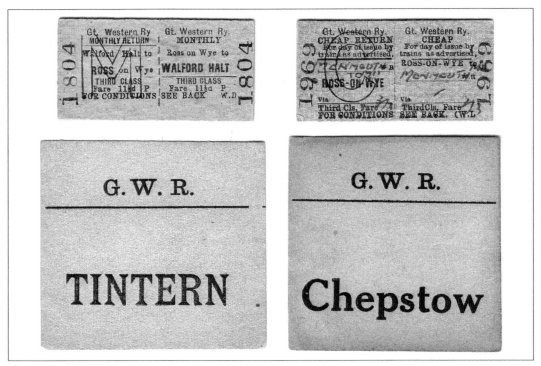

Two tickets from the Ross & Monmouth Railway's line during Great Western days, and a pair of GWR luggage labels for trunks and suitcases dispatched to stations on the lower reaches of the Wye.

3

A Very English River

From Hay to Hereford, a distance of thirty-six miles, the journey can
be performed by boat, and those who can afford the time will be well
repaid both by the scenery and the number of places of historic
interest which are passed.

(*The Wye Valley. From Plynlimon to Hereford*, Great Western Railway, 1923)

Leaving Hay, the Wye Valley Walk follows the Wye eastwards on its southern side
to Bredwardine, though taking a much more direct line than the meandering river.

A multi-view card featuring Hereford. (*Unidentified*)

Just over the English border from Hay is the village of Whitney-on-Wye, with its famous Rhydspence Inn. Originally a fourteenth-century manor house, by Tudor times it was a drovers' inn and today incorporates a hotel and restaurant, thus keeping the old tradition alive. The postcard's sender (in 1951) has written: 'Here is a photo of the little Inn we are staying in, claims to be 600 years old. It is charming here & the country is wonderfully beautiful & the food excellent. Very noisy on Sunday evening when all the Welsh come over the border to booze.' Wales was of course famously 'dry' on Sundays at that time, hence the exodus! (*Frith's Series*)

Closer to Hereford is Bredwardine, where an elegant brick bridge – the only such on the Wye – was built in 1769 as a toll bridge to replace a pair of ferries. It was also the only bridge on the upper Wye to survive the great flood of 1795. (*Wilson-Phillips, Hereford*)

The parish church of St Andrew's, Bredwardine, midway between Hay and Hereford on the south bank of the river. The famous diarist, Francis Kilvert, was vicar here from November 1877 until his death in September 1879. A bridge trustee, he recorded in his diary in December 1878 that 'huge masses and floes of ice were coming down the river all day, rearing, crushing and thundering against the bridge.' It did not fail that time either. Finally rebuilt in the early 1920s, it is a remarkable survivor. (*1 East St, Hereford*)

The Wye Valley Walk crosses the Wye from west to east via Bredwardine bridge and then takes a direct path north of the winding river.

Almost at the very end of its eastwards detour, the Wye reaches Hereford. This is the old road bridge which, dating from 1490, is the oldest on the river. It replaced an eleventh-century wooden structure and has, as is only to be expected, been repaired, widened and strengthened many times. One noteworthy incident during that long life is that in 1645 it was partly blown up by the city's besieged Royalist garrison. (*The Photochrom Co. Ltd., London & Tunbridge Wells*)

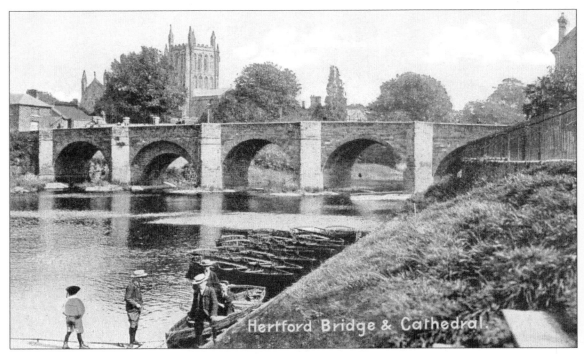

An earlier view of the bridge, with an Edwardian family apparently having just enjoyed a boating excursion on the river. Note the wrong place name in the printed caption – a not uncommon postcard printer's error. (*Delittle, Fenwick & Co., York, for the Christian Novels Publishing Co.*)

Another Edwardian card of the same Hereford scene – moonlit postcard views were commonly produced if the location, as here, was deemed picturesque enough. (*The 'D.F. & Co.' Series, Delittle, Fenwick & Co., York*)

The bridge from the southern bank, looking upstream. The more rounded arch on the left is the one destroyed in 1645. (*'Princess Novels' Series*)

Looking westwards from before the road bridge towards Hunderton Bridge. This is a Great Western Railway structure of 1912/13, built of steel arches on masonry pillars. It replaced an earlier (1853) iron bridge, utilising the same piers, and carried a goods line into the city off the existing main line from Abergavenny. It closed in 1966 and now carries a footpath and cycleway. (*Frith's Series, F. Frith & Co. Ltd., Reigate*)

After Bredwardine the Wye Valley Walk largely abandons the river, wandering through a succession of small villages, but rejoins it 2 miles west of Hereford, then crosses from the north bank to the south via Hunderton Bridge.

A similar view upstream, from slightly nearer the old road bridge; the boats for hire on the left bank in both views are testament to the enduring popularity of 'messing about on the river'. Between Hunderton Bridge and the old road bridge a new concrete crossing carrying the A49, Greyfriars Bridge, was added in 1966 to ease congestion in the city centre. (*The Milton 'Bromo' Series. Woolstone Bros, London E.C.*)

From the old road bridge eastwards is a delightful riverside walk through Bishop's Meadow, affording fine views of the cathedral and the bishop's palace on the opposite bank of the Wye. Over the years it has been gradually tidied up, and is no longer as natural-looking as seen here. (*Harvey Barton & Son, Ltd., Bristol*)

Hereford Cathedral, on the north bank of the Wye. As is also the case at Worcester on the Severn, the cathedral was sited on ground just high enough to escape all but the most severe of floods, but very close to the river in order to facilitate the delivery of building materials. In 1952 the sender of the postcard obviously made a special journey here for she has written: 'We are here for the day it is lovely. We had a lovely service in the Cathedral.' (*Photochrom Co. Ltd., Graphic Studios, Tunbridge Wells, Kent*)

Hereford Cathedral, as an institution, dates from Saxon times and was founded at the shrine of St Ethelbert, a king of East Anglia murdered by his overlord Offa (of Offa's Dyke fame). It was rebuilt between 1074 and 1145 by the Normans, though the massive central tower dates from about 1315. It once carried a wooden spire, encased in lead, though this was removed in 1790. (*Wilson-Phillips*)

The cathedral also once sported a western tower, but this collapsed in 1786, damaging much of the nave. Fears of a similar occurrence were possibly the reason for the removal of the central spire four years later. (*Frith's Series, F. Frith & Co. Ltd. Reigate*)

Hereford Cathedral's famous upper-room chained library, so-called because the books are literally chained to their shelves. This was standard practice in medieval times, as hand-written tomes – or even early printed ones – were incredibly valuable and had to be protected against theft. This rare surviving example of such a library, together with the more famous and even rarer Mappa Mundi, is now exhibited in a new home at the west end of the cathedral, completed in 1996 and funded by the philanthropist Sir Paul Getty. (*Photochrom Co. Ltd., London and Tunbridge Wells*)

Looking eastwards from the cathedral tower towards Castle Green (left) and Victoria Bridge; the road bridge is just out of the picture to the right. This view is remarkably unaltered today, the major difference now being the presence of an avenue of mature trees on the right-hand river bank. (*Exclusive Celesque Series, Photochrom Co. Ltd., London and Tunbridge Wells*)

At the end of the riverside walk is Victoria Bridge, designed by the City Engineer, John Parker, to commemorate the 1897 Diamond Jubilee of Queen Victoria. It opened the following year and connects the Wye's south bank with Castle Green, the site of Hereford Castle. It replaced a ferry, itself only five years old. (*Harvey Barton & Son, Ltd., Bristol*)

Victoria Bridge again, and the north bank walk laid to serve it, at a time when it was still young enough to be deemed the 'new' bridge. (Unidentified)

The Wye Valley Walk crosses via Victoria Bridge then bears left to cut off a large loop in the river before paralleling, then rejoining, it.

A similar, but slightly later view of the Victoria Bridge; railings have now been added to the path to stop people falling – or diving – into the water. Seemingly placid, the river can be quite treacherous here and numerous drownings have occurred over the years. Again, the cathedral dominates the skyline despite its comparatively low situation. This remains the case today, the city being virtually unsullied by modern high-rise buildings. (*T. Harding Son & Co's Bristol Real Photo Series*)

Victoria Bridge again, in this photograph at a time of very low water. The ornate finials on top of the four suspension towers have since disappeared, and the original timber deck was replaced in 1968 by one of galvanised steel covered in asphalt. The wrought-ironwork is still very much the original though, and was manufactured by the firm of Findlay & Co. of Motherwell. (*Real Photo Series, C.E.S. Hereford*)

The preaching cross standing amid the ruins of Hereford's Dominican or Blackfriars friary, its location being in Coningsby Street midway between the railway station and Hereford United's football ground. (Dominicans were known commonly as 'black friars' on account of the black mantles they wore.) The ruins date from the fourteenth century and are next to the 1614 Coningsby Hospital, an almshouse for old soldiers which incorporates a Knights of St John of Jerusalem dining hall of about 1170. (*Boots Cash Chemist 'Pelham' Series*)

The River Walk between Castle Green and the cathedral, in the landscaped gardens set several feet above the level of the river. This and the following two postcards form an overlapping panorama of the gardens this side of the river. (*Wilson & Phillips*)

Castle Green marks the extent of the old castle bailey. The original structure was Saxon, built to protect the city against the Welsh, but was later rebuilt and enlarged from Norman times onwards. During the 1645 siege of the city it was held successfully by the Royalists after which time, as with so many castles that had outlived their usefulness, it fell into ruin with the masonry stolen for reuse elsewhere. (*Celesque Series, Photochrom Co. Ltd., London and Tunbridge Wells*)

Further round Castle Green, looking away from the river. The monument is to Admiral Nelson, celebrating his victory at the Battle of Trafalgar. (*Wilson & Phillips*)

The sender's message here, in 1908, is: 'Came down here on Friday. Having delightful weather as am able to get about on my bike. Did 28 mls yesterday & 18 on Sat.' (*Frith's Series, F. Frith & Co. Ltd. Reigate*)

The Castle Green end of Victoria Bridge, this time looking down the river. Beyond the trees on the south bank are the outlying districts of Putson and Lower Bullingham. (*Harvey Barton and Son Ltd., Bristol*)

Hereford's new Town Hall in St Owen Street, built in 1904 to the designs of Henry Cheers, a late-Victorian architect who excelled in designing municipal buildings with all the ostentation beloved of the civic dignitaries of his time, in towns and cities both large and small. (*F. Frith & Co., Ltd. Reigate*)

Another unmistakable building in Hereford is the Old House, a preserved 1621 half-timbered structure once home to the Butchers Guild; it stands in the open space known as High Town in the centre of the city. Since 1929 it has housed a small museum based around how its rooms would have looked in Jacobean times. Beyond is All Saints' church, with its twisted spire – and possessor of another chained library. (*W. Hagelberg, London*)

The Old House from the other, western end, looking towards the twelfth-century St Peter's church (differentiated from All Saints' by the tall finials on the corners of its tower). The Old House was once one of several in Butchers' Row, though probably the grandest as befitting its guild status; it is certainly one of the finest surviving Jacobean townhouses in the country. (*Valentine's Series*)

An idealised, 'chocolate box' painting of the Old House, reproduced as an Edwardian postcard. Before its new life as a museum, it was the premises of Lloyds Bank. Today, in a pedestrianised area surrounded by modern shopfronts and signs, it looks even more incongruous than on these postcards. (*'Facsimile' Series, S. Hildesheimer, & Co., Ltd. London & Manchester. Views of Hereford Series*)

High Town in the days before the First World War, looking towards the Old House and St Peter's church. This large open space was a natural and ideal focus for the city's economic life with its 900-year tradition of commerce continuing right up to the present. The medieval stalls and booths have been replaced by modern shops and stores – except on market and fair days of course, though the modern fairs are most definitely of the 'fun' kind. (*The Wrench Series*)

Virtually the same view, this time three decades or so later with the horse and cart having given way to the internal combustion engine and the bicycle. The motor coach in the foreground belongs to Black & White Motorways Ltd of Cheltenham Spa, and is presumably here on an excursion or tour of some kind. Note the roof rack for the stowing of passengers' luggage in all weathers – not an uncommon practice in early motoring days, even on cars. (*Photochrom Co. Ltd., Royal Tunbridge Wells*)

Broad Street lies west of High Town and runs from All Saints' church towards the cathedral and thence to Bridge Street. As its name indicates, it is a wide thoroughfare and and deliberately made so for the purpose of driving cattle up from the river crossing into the market. (*Coloured Enamelette View Series, Gibson Bros & Co., London E.C.*)

Broad Street at a later date. As with the pair of cards on the opposite page, this lower one records the abrupt arrival in the city, after centuries of horse-drawn traffic, of the motor car. From here on the traditional cart or wagon would be relegated to such mundane tasks as the delivery of milk or the collection of scrap metal. (*Unidentified*)

The much-photographed Broad Street again, this time on a 1941-franked postcard. The 1930s cars and vans serve to emphasise just how wide the street is: six of them could line up abreast with no difficulty at all. The horse and cart has not disappeared entirely though – there is one at the kerb behind the van on the right, while on the corner is parked a small motorbike complete with the front fairings typical of the period, designed to protect the rider's legs – a feature later adopted by motor scooter manufacturers. (*Charles E. Brumwell, Bookseller, Hereford*)

4

The Romantic Wye

The portion of the Wye Valley which lies between Hereford and
Ross must be regarded as a prelude to that supremely impressive
scenery which is to be found on either side of "the bounteous river"
between Ross and its junction with the great tidal stream the "Severn Sea".
(*The Wye Valley. From Hereford to Chepstow*, Great Western Railway, 1923)

The Wye Valley Walk leaves Hereford along the east bank, but at Hampton Bishop
deviates from the meandering river to continue on through a succession of villages.

A multi-view postcard with scenes of Ross-on-Wye. (*Unidentified*)

TOUR OF THE WYE.

From Hay and Hereford to . . . .
Ross, Monmouth, Tintern, Chepstow,

AND ALL PARTS OF THE WYE.

Experienced Watermen.

J. JORDAN,

Boats and Punts built to order.   BOAT BUILDER AND PROPRIETOR.

Wye Bridge, HEREFORD.

The volume of pleasure boating on the Wye has always been limited in comparison with that on the Severn, and was largely confined to the hiring-out of small rowing boats at various locations (evidence of which can be seen on many of the cards reproduced here). Before the First World War however longer excursions were on offer, as this advertisement from a 1900s *'Borough' Guide* to Hereford demonstrates – though the claim to reach 'all parts of the Wye' was no more accurate then as it would be today!

ON THE WYE AT PUTSON, HEREFORD.

One mile south of Hereford is the district of Putson. Now very much a built-up suburb of the city, sandwiched between the Wye to the north and the railway line to Abergavenny to the south, it was far more rural in nature when this card was posted in 1908. (*Wilson & Phillips*)

Before the First World War, organised excursions by road to beauty spots were largely catered for by horse-drawn charabancs. After the war motorised versions of these vehicles quickly superseded them, offering a far greater range of travel within the same time constraints. This advertisement, from the 1923 official guide to Hereford, is for such a service operated by a private garage – one of hundreds of similar businesses across the country seizing the opportunity offered by the availability of suitable vehicles from manufacturers no longer geared up to supplying the war effort (see also p. 83).

The next town on the Wye – once more heading more or less due south – is Ross-on-Wye. Five miles north-west of there on the west bank is the village of Hoarwithy, famous for its lavishly ornate hilltop parish church designed by J.P. Seddon and funded by the incumbent, the Revd William Poole, during the latter half of the nineteenth century. Decorated in the most extravagant manner with marble, lapis lazuli and mosaics, it boasts an open exterior cloister and a Romanesque campanile – seen here in the centre – most out of place in an English country churchyard! (*Unidentified*)

Between Hoarwithy and Ross the Wye Valley Walk rejoins the river's east bank at How Caple.

Ross-on-Wye is mentioned in the Domesday Book as a village and manor of the Bishop of Hereford, with a saw mill. This view of the river, looking almost south across the loop it makes here, was a popular one for photographers, their vantage point today being the location of a boathouse. Alas, more mundane rowboats – and coracles – are seldom seen on much of the river now. (*F. Frith & Co. Ltd., Reigate*)

Ross from across the river, with the spire of St Mary's again dominating the skyline. The sandstone tower in the centre – an eighteenth-century folly known as the Gazebo – is now a private house, while the white building by the riverside is the Hope & Anchor pub. The tall central building looking like a warehouse is actually a school. (*Valentine's Series*)

Ross from Red Hill, above the town on the old coach road to Monmouth, looking towards the same school seen above. The town's location at the head of the narrowing valley below it gave rise to its nickname of 'Gateway to the Wye Valley'. (*F. Frith & Co. Ltd., Reigate*)

St Mary's church, dating from 1280 but with a later tower and 205ft-high spire. The tall cross in the foreground is a monument to the town's plague victims. (*F. Frith and Co., Ltd., Reigate*)

Looking from the churchyard across to the Rudhall Almshouses. Founded in the fourteenth century and rebuilt in Tudor times, the almshouses were restored in 1960 and the original five dwellings converted into three. (*F. Frith & Co., Ltd., Reigate*)

This is the Plague Cross in Ross churchyard. Its original inscription – *Plague Ano Dom 1637 Burials 315 Libera nos Domine* – is illegible today but has been augmented by a nearby plaque, which reads: 'This cross was erected as a memorial to 315 people who died in Ross during the plague of 1637 and who were buried at night without coffins. Libera Nos Domine.' (*The 'Wyndham' Series*)

A famous feature of St Mary's for many years were the elm trees growing inside the church – two by the window at the east end and one by the north wall of the transept. They sprang from suckers from an avenue of elms planted outside in 1684 by John Kyle (1637–1724), a local philanthropist honoured as 'The Man of Ross'. During a restoration project in 1878 the trees were felled and the suckers died off but were not removed until 1953 when they were found to be infested with woodworm. They have now been replaced by a vine. (*F. Frith & Co., Ltd., Reigate*)

The Valley Hotel in Edde Cross Street, Ross. This began life as a row of Georgian houses that were later knocked through and given a mock-Tudor façade as an unlicensed hotel. The Gazebo seen earlier was in the gardens behind it. It has now reverted to being a row of private dwellings. Opposite is the more elegant Swan Hotel; this once boasted its own garage – note the petrol pump on the pavement bottom left, once a fairly common sight in towns and villages. (*Harvey Barton & Son Ltd, Bristol*)

The town's impressive Market Hall, built of red sandstone in about 1650 and still in use today as a centrepiece for the regular markets. The immediate surroundings have been pedestrianised now, though. (*Raphael Tuck & Sons 'O'er Hill and Dale' Post Card, 'The Wye Valley'*)

Also little altered is the view through the arches of the Market Hall down Broad Street towards the now-closed railway station. As its name suggests, Broad Street was one of the town's principal thoroughfares then as now. In fact, apart from the visual cues offered by the motor cars, the view looks very much the same today. (*F. Frith & Co., Ltd., Reigate*)

The Chase Hotel, one of Ross-on-Wye's premier hotels, overlooking the river close to the town centre. Formerly a Georgian country house, it stands in 11 acres of landscaped gardens. (*Frith's Series*)

The Chase Hotel again: the front from the driveway . . . (*F. Frith & Co., Ltd., Reigate*)

. . . and inside the grand entrance hall. (*F. Frith & Co., Ltd., Reigate*)

ROSS-ON-WYE.

WESTFIELD

Charmingly Situated

SMALL PRIVATE HOTEL.

OVERLOOKING River Every Comfort and Consideration for Visitors.

Garage. Moderate Terms.

MR. & MRS. J. L. PEMBRIDGE.

On the WYE VALLEY TOUR Stop at

ROSS

FOR MORNING COFFEE, LUNCHEONS AND TEAS.
HOME-MADE DAINTIES A SPECIALITY.

THE KIT-KAT TEA ROOMS
AND BOARD-RESIDENCE.
(NEXT DOOR G.P. OFFICE).
OPEN ON SUNDAYS 3.30—7.30, SUMMER SEASON,
Where you will find installed the latest Soda Fountain & Delicious Ices.
VEGETARIANS CATERED FOR.

Telegrams and Telephone 122 Ross.   OPEN 9 a.m.—9 p.m.

SYMOND'S YAT.

The PADDOCKS HOTEL
R.A.C., A.A.

DELIGHTFULLY Situated, with South Aspect. The only Hotel with Uninterrupted View of Gorge. Electric Light and Central Heating. H. & C. Running Water. **25** Bedrooms. Tennis, Clock Golf, Fishing, Shooting. Dairy Farm attached, with Own Produce.

E. A. LEWIS, PROPRIETRESS.

'Phone, Whitchurch Ross **39.**   Tels., " Paddocks."

Hotels, guest houses and other establishments in the Wye Valley were keen to attract visitors, and advertisements such as these were commonly placed in all manner of guidebooks from the late nineteenth century onwards. Typically, they would proclaim their best, or even exclusive, features in order to outdo their rivals. (*From the Ward, Lock publication cited on p. 128*)

Another view of Broad Street, again from the Market Hall, this time in the pre-motor car age. Besides leading towards the railway station, this was and is one of the principal ways out of the town for roads to the north and the east. (*F. Frith & Co., Ltd., Reigate*)

The Wye Valley Walk enters Ross along the river bank from the north, passes through the town and heads directly south towards Goodrich, cutting off another long, winding stretch of the river.

Although the appearance of Ross was 'improved' during the mid-nineteenth century with mock-Gothic town walling and the like, this point on the river was defended by the genuine Wilton Castle in the district of that name on the opposite, western bank. Dating from the thirteenth century, it was converted into a country house in the late sixteenth; razed during the Civil War, a new house was built within the ruins in the nineteenth century. The district also lends its name to the stone bridge believed to date from 1597, built as a toll bridge to replace a ferry. (*E.S. London*)

Wilton Bridge was for many centuries the only road bridge connecting Ross with the land west of the Wye, until, that is, the 1960 opening of the new A40 bypass to the north of the town. Indeed, it was for many years one of only two in the county on the river, a vital link between South Wales and Hereford on one side, and Gloucester and all points east to London on the other. It has had an eventful life, having been blown up in the Civil War, damaged in the great flood of 1795, and strengthened and widened during the twentieth century. It still sports this impressive sundial in the downstream central refuge – once of great benefit to travellers, but now a fascinating curiosity. Not unnaturally, it displays local time, some 10 or 12 minutes behind GMT. (*F. Frith & Co. Ltd., Reigate*)

The Wye doubles back briefly on itself at Ross, in a long curve of the type commonly known as a horseshoe bend on account of its distinctive shape. The rural landscape captured here is today rather more encroached upon by modern developments. (*Tilley & Son, Publishers, Ledbury*)

The bend again, as seen from the eastern bank, with Wilton Bridge out of sight in the trees in the far left at the point where the river starts to turn back southwards. (*Lawrence & Fowler, Printers, Ross*)

The Birmingham & Midland Motor Omnibus Co. Ltd (founded 1904), was a concern better known for many decades across the western half of central England by its trading names of 'Midland' and later 'Midland Red' (after the colour of its vehicles). It opened its first Hereford garage, in the yard of the Black Lion in Bridge Street in 1920 and soon absorbed – or put out of business – local rivals such as that of St George's Garage (see the advertisement on p. 69 from the same publication).

The next crossing point on the Wye below Ross is Kerne Bridge, said by some to be the most beautiful on the whole river. Built as a toll bridge in 1828 by B.D. Jones, in different coloured sandstones, it replaced an ancient ferry nearly half a mile upstream. Today it carries the B4229 connecting the A40 from Ross to Monmouth, west of the river, with the B4228 on the eastern side. The view is looking north, with the Great Western's Kerne Bridge station on the right. Opened in 1873 by the Ross & Monmouth Railway, the station closed in 1959. (*Valentine's Series*)

The Wye Valley Walk joins the river here from the north and crosses via Kerne Bridge;
it then follows the southern bank closely to Welsh Bicknor.

Goodrich Castle, Ross-on-Wye.

On the other side of the river from Kerne Bridge station stand the picturesque ruins of Goodrich Castle, now in the care of English Heritage. (*Unidentified*)

Goodrich Castle, as a fortified site, dates from at least the late eleventh century, when it was known as Godric's Castle. What stand today, though, are the remains of its twelfth-century rebuild, including the square Norman keep seen here. It is thought that it was never attacked in medieval times and not until 1646, when it was isolated as the last Royalist stronghold in Herefordshire, did the castle come under any serious threat. The armaments of the time proved too powerful for the ancient structure and it was captured and 'slighted' – damaged beyond use – by Parliamentary forces under Colonel John Birch. (*H.M. Office of Works, Rembrandt Intaglio Printing Co. Ltd., London*)

A wonderful view of the castle in its early twentieth-century 'romantic', overgrown state – a condition that would certainly not be tolerated today. (*'Kromo' Series, B. & D. London E.C.*)

Some 2 miles downstream of Kerne Bridge, on a peninsula formed by another great horseshoe bend in the river, is the tiny settlement of Welsh Bicknor. Its name reflects the fact that this was once in a detached portion of Monmouthshire, and served to distinguish it from the much larger English Bicknor a mile or so south of it, across and away from the river in Gloucestershire on the edge of the Forest of Dean. (*F. Frith & Co. Ltd., Reigate*)

At Welsh Bicknor the Wye Valley Walk crosses the river on the disused Lydbrook Junction railway bridge, then follows closely its eastern bank all the way to and through Symonds Yat.

A multi-view card of the next stretch of the Wye, undoubtedly the most visually impressive reach of the whole river. The cards following, portraying the various features of Symonds Yat, are not presented in a strict linear order; instead they are grouped by subject for ease of recognition. (*Valentine's*)

After the loop at Welsh Bicknor, the river heads south-west for about a mile before doubling back on itself once more, this time heading due north at the start of an even greater horseshoe bend. On the western heights nearly 400ft above the river at the start of this bend, on the crest of the narrow neck of the loop, is the vantage point known as Symonds Yat, or simply Yat Rock. (*F. Frith & Co., Ltd., Reigate*)

A similar view to the previous one, though the portrait format of the postcard frames the scene more effectively as the river heads back north almost to Goodrich before it starts to slowly swing westward. 'Yat' is a local name for a gate or, by extension, a pass and 'Symonds' is from Robert Symonds, a seventeenth-century Sheriff of Herefordshire and local landowner. As well as a vantage point for enjoying the outstanding vistas unfolding in all directions, Yat Rock is an ideal spot for watching the kestrels, ravens and buzzards that frequent the valley here. Lower down, kingfishers are to be seen skimming the river in their quest for food. (*Unidentified*)

After the Wye has turned back south, round the 450ft high point of Huntsham Hill, it reaches the settlement of Symonds Yat, divided by the river into Symonds Yat East in Gloucestershire and, seen here looking back north, Symonds Yat West in Herefordshire. (*Unidentified*)

Symonds Yat West again, this time looking in the opposite direction downstream towards Monmouth. (Note the slight overlap with the houses bottom right here and bottom left in the card above.) Just discernible to the left of the river is the railway that once threaded the gorge, its trackbed now utilised by the Wye Valley Walk. (*Unidentified*)

Yat Rock again: the portrait format of the postcard emphasises the impressive nature of the scene. Old cards of the Symonds Yat area are commonly found, a century later, in almost every postcard dealer's stock, such was the vast number of them produced for sale at this much-visited location. Many, like this one, were never posted – evidence that they were bought as souvenirs for putting in albums. The cottage shown here is tucked into the side of Codwall Rocks, over which towers Yat Rock itself. (*Unidentified*)

The view from Yat Rock, looking back eastwards towards Welsh Bicknor. Not surprisingly, given its intimate nature with the gorge, the railway appears in many views of Symonds Yat. The line was opened by the Ross & Monmouth Railway, to connect the two towns of its title, in 1873; as with many of the small companies of the region, it was worked by the Great Western until eventually absorbed by it in 1922 when the whole of the national network was rationalised. (*'Sepiatype Series', Valentine's*)

Symond's Yat station (note the official spelling) was opened on 1 August 1873 and closed 5 January 1959 – the same time as Kerne Bridge – when the line shut. It was sited in Symonds Yat East, due south of Yat Rock under which it passed in a tunnel. Three shires are in view: Hereford on the right, Gloucester on the left and Monmouth straight ahead. (*Harvey Barton & Son Ltd., Bristol*)

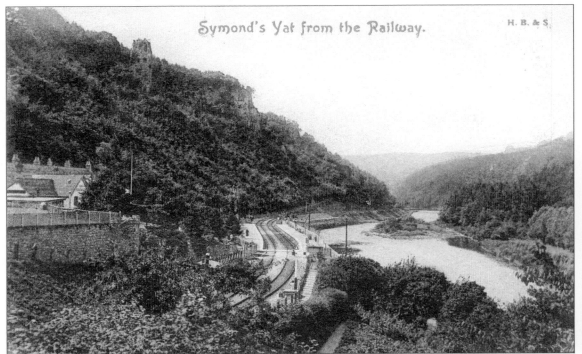

A general view of the station again, this card being one that was sent to Newport in Monmouthshire on 9 August 1905. The message is brief and to the point: 'Arrived so far in good time.' (*H.B. & S.*)

The station seen from the opposite direction. The small island in the foreground can be seen in many postcards of Symonds Yat, and provides a useful point of reference when trying to identify precise locations. (*Valentine's Series*)

A delightful photographic postcard capturing the view looking north from the station, with a train just emerging from the single-track tunnel. (*Tilley & Son, Ledbury*)

The Wye Valley Walk, following the river bank in from the north, now occupies the old railway trackbed on its way south.

An unusual view of the station, looking down from one of the cliffside walks. Symond's Yat was a passing place on the railway, complete with two platforms; the point at which the track singled again at the other end of the station from the tunnel can just be seen. (*Mrs L. Goulder, Whitchurch*)

Ye Olde Ferrie Inne, with the mock-medieval spelling of its name a deliberate attempt to lure in those tourists in search of an authentic 'historical experience'. The location is upstream in Symonds Yat West, just where the gorge sides close in dramatically. The age-old rope ferry is seen in action – indeed, much as it can be seen today. (*Unidentified*)

There is a second rope ferry on the Wye here, based at the sixteenth-century Saracen's Head in Symonds Yat East a few hundred yards downstream of the other. Both are worked by the ferryman employing a simple hand-over-hand pulling action on the rope strung across the river. The view is from the west bank towards the inn, the second and third buildings from the left. In front of the inn is a terraced area overlooking the river, complete with tables and sunshades. (*English Series, Photo-Precision Ltd., St Albans*)

A closer look at the Saracen's Head Inn, though at this earlier date it is obscured by a great deal of foliage that was cleared later. The slipway for the ferry is on the far left of the scene; the building above it appears on several of the cards here and will be seen again later. (*Unidentified*)

Looking towards the Saracen's Head and its neighbouring buildings from a little way upstream. Immediately downstream of the inn is the railway station. On back of this card, posted in 1910, the sender has written: 'Another view of the river where we were boating on Thursday.' (*Valentine's Series*)

Looking towards the railway station, centre, from the riverside building with the fake half-timbering, its identity now revealed as a tea-room catering for visitors not wishing to partake of something stronger in the Saracen's Head next door. (*English Series, Photo-Precision Ltd., St Albans*)

The hillside above the Saracen's Head; the grand house, centre, somewhat incongruously named the Chalet, would have enjoyed unsurpassed views up and down the river – unless the trees on the neighbouring properties grew too high! Its elevated position also made it quite safe from any risk of flooding. (*Unidentified*)

The Wye Rapids Hotel was for many years a distinctive landmark building in Symonds Yat West, enjoying an elevated position on the hillside directly opposite Yat Rock. Sadly, it was demolished in 1998 and replaced by eighteen holiday cottages. It is seen here from Yat Rock, the perspective of the photograph giving the viewer a good idea of the commanding position of the vantage point on this side of the crest as well. (*English Series, Photo-Precision Ltd., St Albans*)

The Paddocks Hotel, in contrast, is still in business. It stands at the entrance to the gorge, high up on the west bank on the B4164 into Symonds Yat West off the A40 at Whitchurch. Its appearance has changed markedly over the years, as this and the postcard below clearly show. (*Valentine's 'Carbo Colour' Postcards, Valentine & Sons Ltd., Dundee and London*)

The Paddocks Hotel again, looking much as it does today. The view in both cases is towards the north-east, across the great loop of the (invisible) Wye. (*Barrows Press Ltd., Printers, Cheltenham*)

The Wye Rapids Hotel again, this time photographed from a much lower position on the opposite side of the river. (*English Series, Photo-Precision Ltd., St Albans*)

The River, Symonds Yat.

As indicated by an earlier card, boating was a popular activity at Symonds Yat for, despite the river being in a narrow gorge, it normally flowed quite placidly. This location, where rowboats and punts are obviously for hire, cannot be located precisely . . . (*Unidentified*)

BOATING PLACE, RIVER YAT.

. . . though this one can: note the station fence on the left. Today's visitors are more likely to forego any physical effort and instead opt for one of the river cruises currently offered by three operators, though modern-style canoeing and kayaking are popular. (*Valentine's 'Sepiatype' Series*)

More boating, on a 1910-franked postcard, at the same location as that shown at the top of the previous page. Directly above the boats is what appears to be a large boathouse, possibly used for winter storage and repairs. (*S.D. Real Photo Series*)

Once again, the precise location of this pleasant scene has so far proved impossible to find with certainty. (*Valentine 'Carbo Colour' Postcards*)

A last look at the Olde Ferrie Inne and its surroundings, looking downstream. (*F. Frith & Co. Ltd., Reigate*)

On the same side of the river, a last look at Symonds Yat West. The Great Doward of the caption is the name of the hill behind the village, on the lower slopes of which it clings. (*Valentine's 'Sepiatype' Series*)

South of Symonds Yat the river doubles back northwards; at the southernmost point of this bend the Wye Valley Walk crosses over from the railway formation via a 1957 Forestry Commission footbridge, then follows the western bank all the way to Monmouth.

As the river turns south again, it passes beneath the shadow of the Seven Sisters on the western bank, this being the fanciful name given to the outcropping rocky pinnacles on the cliff face in the distance. This view is looking downstream . . . (*Unidentified*)

. . . and this one looking back, from downstream of the rocks, in the direction of Symonds Yat. Although astonishing in scale and appearance, the whole gorge was formed by a simple geological process: the river eroded the rising land faster than it rose, so carving its way through it. (*Valentine's*)

5

The Monmouthshire Wye

Sixteen miles divide Monmouth from Chepstow, and a short distance below the town, which has been described on excellent authority as "delightsome", the hills, which break away at Monmouth, once more come together, forming a second gorge through which the stream winds towards the Severn.

(*The Wye Valley. From Hereford to Chepstow*, Great Western Railway, 1923)

The Wye Valley Walk enters Monmouthshire a short distance above Monmouth, following the west bank of the river.

A multi-view card featuring scenes of Monmouth.
(*English Series, Photo-Precision Ltd., St Albans*)

Another Monmouth multi-view card. 'Good Luck' cards of this type are commonly found, with a black cat or a horseshoe in the centre. Other multi-views, usually from seaside resorts, often sport messages along the lines of 'Just Arrived At' or 'Having A Great Time At'. The town's most famous son is perhaps the twelfth-century Welsh chronicler (and later Bishop of St Asaph) Geoffrey of Monmouth, though the future Henry V of England is thought to have been born here, in 1387, in the castle. (*Valentine's*)

Looking from the east bank of the Wye across the river to the town, with the spire of St Mary's church, on the site of a former Benedictine priory, rising above the houses. To the left, between the trees, can be glimpsed the arches of the Wye Bridge. (*F. Frith & Co. Ltd., Reigate*)

Monmouth's Wye Bridge is believed to date from 1617, though it was widened in 1879, and carries the A466 on what is the town's only road crossing of the river. In a very real sense it embodies the unchanging nature of this border town, a solid stone testament to the fact that many of the excesses of the twentieth century – architectural or otherwise – have largely passed it by. (*Chrome-Series, Jarrold & Sons, Ltd. Norwich, England*)

The Wye Valley Walk crosses to the eastern river bank via the Wye Bridge.

Monmouth derives its name from the River Monnow, or Afon Mynwy, which joins the Wye just below the town, with the old settlement – including an early twelfth-century castle – being sited on the tongue of land between the two waterways. The thirteenth-century Monnow Bridge, which replaced an earlier timber structure, crosses the Monnow a little way above the mouth of that river, and boasts a unique surviving example in Britain of a fortified gateway on a bridge. (*Salmon Series, J. Salmon Ltd., Sevenoaks*)

A closer look at the Monnow Bridge's massive gateway, a relic of more turbulent times designed and built, complete with a portcullis, in order to repel invaders – English or Welsh. The two gentlemen captured by the camera on this occasion would appear to pose no discernible threat. Known as the Monnow Gate, it is the only one of the town's original four defensive gateways that survives. It was not that effective a deterrent though – the Monnow could easily be forded upstream! It proved of more use as a toll house and a guard room for the local militia. (*Excel Series*)

One of Monmouth's curious features is this projecting window in Priory Street near the church. It is named Geoffrey's Window after Geoffrey of Monmouth, the building incorporating it being formerly a nineteenth-century schoolroom housed in a much-rebuilt portion of the town's old priory. (*Hartmann*)

GENERAL VIEW OF MONMOUTH FROM PENALT. (11)   G.128.

Looking back at Monmouth from below the town. Here the river was crossed by two railway bridges, the further one in the photograph being a three-span truss-girder structure opened in 1874 by the Ross & Monmouth Railway and the nearer one, complete with its impressive masonry viaduct across the flood plain, a single-span lattice-girder bridge opened in 1861 by the grandly named Coleford, Monmouth, Usk & Pontypool Railway. (*Valentine's*)

Both the railway companies mentioned above were absorbed into the Great Western Railway, their lines later becoming part of British Railways. The 1861 bridge was closed with its line in 1964 and the span removed; the 1874 structure fared better, however, for although its line closed in 1959, the bridge still stands intact. (*Celesque Series, The Photochrom Co. Ltd., London and Tunbridge Wells*)

River Wye at Redbrook. (Monmouth.)

Below Monmouth the valley sides start to close in and after some 2 miles the settlement of Redbrook (Upper and Lower) is reached. Here there is another former railway bridge, this one having been built by the Wye Valley Railway in 1876 to carry its line between Monmouth and Chepstow from east to west across the river. A footway was added to the bridge in 1955, and after the line was closed by British Railways nine years later it remained open for walkers. ('*Weekly Tale-Teller*' *Postcard, Delittle, Fenwick and Co., York*)

The Wye Valley Walk crosses to the western bank of the river via the Redbrook Bridge.

LLANDOGO. ON THE WYE.

Next on our journey down the river comes the small village of Llandogo. The view here is looking north away from the village, the main settlement being on the hillside behind the camera on the western bank of the river. Just visible running through the fields on the left is the former Wye Valley Railway – another concern absorbed by the Great Western – referred to above. (*The Photochrom Co. Ltd., Graphic Works Tunbridge Wells*)

A similar view to that of the previous card, but from a vantage point even higher up the steep valley side that crowds in here close to the river. Below, the main road (now the A466) and the railway share the flat valley floor with the Wye. (*Walter Scott Bradford*)

Llandogo again, this time looking south to where the floodplain narrows and the road, railway and river are squeezed even more closely together. (*Unidentified*)

The Wye Valley Walk deserts the river 2 miles above Llandogo, bypassing the village to the west, before rejoining it at Brockweir above Tintern.

Below Llandogo is the village of Tintern, which lends its name to its world-famous abbey glimpsed here, in the distance, on the western bank of the river, beyond the Wireworks Bridge. The name of this stone and girder structure is somewhat at odds with the bucolic nature of the scene, for it was erected in 1875 by the Isca Foundry Co. of Newport to connect the local wireworks with the Wye Valley Railway on the opposite side of the river. (*Celesque Series, The Photochrom Co., Ltd., London & Tunbridge Wells*)

Tintern from above the Wireworks Bridge, looking north. Here the houses and main road hug the western bank while the river makes a horseshoe bend around the low-lying land to the east. (*Walter Scott, Bradford*)

The Wireworks Bridge again, viewed from the abbey. Tintern is situated where the fast-flowing Angidy River joins the Wye from the west, a site chosen by the government in 1566 as the perfect place to establish a wire-making industry. It is estimated that by 1821 there were twenty mills on the Angidy, powering a number of industries in addition to the manufacture of wire. Though that industry had died by 1901, the railway lingered on as a horse-worked tramroad until the 1930s; in 1941 the rails were lifted, the bridge eventually enjoying a new lease of life carrying a footpath across the border into Gloucestershire. (*Unidentified*)

A pre-Second World War advertisement for the Beaufort Arms Hotel in Tintern. Though few today would wish to ban the sport of fishing, far fewer would like to see the return of the otter hunts. Thankfully, after facing near-extinction in England, the numbers of these captivating animals are at last increasing – and they have recently returned to the Wye. (*From the Ward, Lock publication cited on p. 128*)

A closer look at the village of Tintern, with its main road constricted by the river on one side and the cliffs on the other leaving only enough room for a single row of houses. Once a centre for brass and iron foundries, today the principal industry is tourism. The sender's message on the back, written in 1923, is in the very best prosaic postcard tradition: 'We are here today & it is lovely having a fine time.' (*Unidentified*)

A closer view of Tintern Abbey, looking north from that same Chepstow road (now the A466). The course of the Wye is just beyond the abbey, the river flowing in the great loop referred to earlier, entering the picture below the steep hillside (centre right) and leaving it immediately to the right of the buildings. (*Unidentified*)

The Wye Valley Walk passes behind the abbey, then turns even further inland, not rejoining the river until just above Chepstow.

By way of contrast, the abbey as seen from the river – before Henry VIII's Dissolution of the Monasteries the river would have been the highway of choice for travellers to and from the abbey, the road (if it had existed at all) being little more than a rocky path. (*E.G. Ballard, Photographer, Welsh Street, Chepstow*)

Tintern Abbey was a Cistercian abbey, founded in 1131 by Walter fitz Richard de Clare, Earl of Chepstow, as the first such in Wales, though the structure that remains dates from the rebuilding programmes of the thirteenth and fourteenth centuries. This period of great economic prosperity, based on agriculture, made it the largest and wealthiest monastic establishment in Wales. After the Dissolution of the Monasteries in 1535 it fell into ruins, unheard of and unvisited until the Romantic movement of the late eighteenth century brought travellers from far and wide to savour its picturesque beauty. (*Unidentified*)

The east window of the abbey. It was with this stretch of the river in mind that one such romantically-minded traveller, the Poet Laureate William Wordsworth, wrote in his poem 'Lines Written a Few miles Above Tintern Abbey, on Revisiting the Banks of the Wye During a Tour, 13 July 1798': 'Once again / Do I behold these steep and lofty cliffs, / Which on a wild secluded scene impress / Thoughts of more deep seclusion; and connect / The landscape with the quiet of the sky.' J.M.W. Turner's painting of the abbey also helped place it firmly on the tourist map. (*E.G. Ballard, Photographer, Welsh Street, Chepstow*)

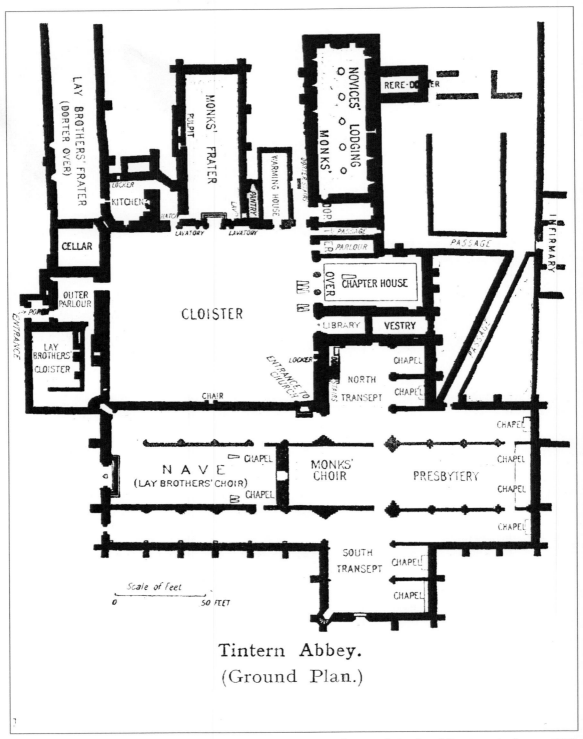

Tintern Abbey.
(Ground Plan.)

The conjectured floorplan of the abbey as it once was, from the Ward, Lock publication cited on p. 128. Tintern is the most complete of all of the ruined abbeys to be found in Wales.

The west front of the abbey. This card and the next (and that of Goodrich Castle on p. 85) were published by His Majesty's Office of Works, the forerunner of today's English Heritage. (*H.M. Office of Works, The Rembrandt Intaglio Printing Co., Ltd., London*)

Tintern Abbey from the south-east. What is clearly evident here – and in the previous pictures – is the astonishing amount of finely carved masonry still surviving in many of the windows. (*H.M. Office of Works, the Rembrandt Intaglio Printing Co. Ld., [sic], London*)

Between Tintern and Chepstow the Wye makes a series of great loops, doubling back on itself on several occasions, making for some dramatic landscape vistas. This is one such, captured by the camera, looking north . . . (*Valentine's Series*)

. . . and this another, as realised in paint by A. de Breanski Jnr, looking towards the mouth of the river with the wide waters of the Severn gleaming below the clouds in the far distance. (*J. Salmon. Sevenoaks, England*)

Midway between Tintern and Chepstow, on the western bank of the Wye, is the high vantage point known as the Wynd Cliff, or simply Wyndcliff, on the A466 shortly after it forsakes the river valley for the higher ground to the west. From here, some 800ft above the river, spectacular views encompassing seven counties can be had to the east and the south – a fact not lost on postcard publishers. (*Valentine's Series*)

The spectacular view from the Wynd Cliff, looking directly south over the great horseshoe loop – the Tidenham Bend – that the Wye makes above Chepstow, with the mouth of the river and shimmering Severn on the far horizon. For the stouter-hearted, the cliff can also be ascended by way of 365 steps cut in 1828 by Osmond Wyatt for the Duke of Beaufort, owner of Chepstow Castle. (*E.G. Ballard, Photographer, Welsh Street, Chepstow*)

An early multi-view card of Chepstow and the Wye Valley above the town, slightly unusual in that it is in portrait format. Chepstow is the last settlement encountered on the river before it joins the Severn and dates from Saxon times, its name simply meaning 'market town', though for many centuries it was an important port (despite having to cope with the 40ft tides of the Severn estuary). The Romans named it Castell Gwent – the latter half of this name being adopted for the old county of Monmouthshire at the time of the ill-advised and much resented 1974 local government reorganisation. (*F. Hartmann's 'Miniature Series'*)

A more orthodox landscape format multi-view card of Chepstow and its surroundings, the centrepiece of the card being the horseshoe bend in the Wye immediately upstream of the town. (*English Series, Photo-Precision Ltd., St Albans*)

In the High Street, looking north towards Beaufort Square, in the centre of Chepstow. It has been remarked in the past that everything in the town is laid out on a slope, and Beaufort Square and its adjoining streets are no exception to the rule, established as they were on the land outside the castle. (*Harvey Barton and Son Ltd., Bristol*)

Beaufort Square again, this time from closer up, still in horse and cart days – and at an unusually traffic-free time of day. A slight slope is discernible even here; as the local eighteenth-century poet the Revd Edward Davies put it, 'Strange to tell, there cannot here be found / One single inch of horizontal ground.' The square is named after the Beaufort Hotel, the coaching inn that once stood here overlooking the town's markets and fairs. (*E.S. London*)

Chepstow High Street, bustling then as now, looking the other way towards the Town Gate. This was one of the entrances in the old town wall (and a toll gate), and was rebuilt in 1524 by the Earl of Worcester, though the windows and 'battlements' are comparatively recent embellishments. (*F. Frith & Co., Ltd., Reigate*)

A later view of this end of the High Street in which minor alterations have been made to the shop frontages, the horse has given way to the motor car, a mass of foliage has been removed from the Council Offices left of the Town Gate – and a bell has been hung above the archway. (*Valentine's*)

A closer view of the Town Gate showing more clearly the pedestrian passageway added on the left-hand side, and the bell. This was formerly the watch bell employed on HMS Chepstow, a First World War paddle-wheel minesweeper built in 1916; it has since been removed and housed in the parish church of St Mary's. The Town Gate was presented to the local council in 1919 by the Duke of Beaufort and currently houses the Town Council offices and Citizen's Advice Bureau in the Gatehouse (left), while the room above the archway is available for meetings, having been variously a prison, a tailor's workshop and a local museum. (*Unidentified*)

Chepstow Castle, in its commanding position on the south bank of the Wye, close to its meeting with the Severn. One of the oldest stone castles in Europe, being originally built of that material, it was begun the year after the Norman Conquest by William fitz Osbern, Earl of Hereford. (*Walter Scott, Bradford*)

The castle was much fought over during the English Civil Wars, and was captured by Parliamentary forces on two separate occasions. State-owned since 1953, it is now in the care of Cadw, the Welsh Assembly's historic environment division. (*Kingsway Real Photo Series*)

The last of the old road bridges across the Wye is that at Chepstow. Built by the Bridgnorth firm of Hazeldine, Rastrick & Brodie and opened in 1816 to replace a succession of wood and stone structures upstream, this is an elegant five-arch bridge of cast-iron. It was reinforced in 1889 and again in 1914 to cope with increasing traffic loads on the A48, the flow eventually being regulated by traffic lights. (*B. Griffiths, Stationer, Chepstow*)

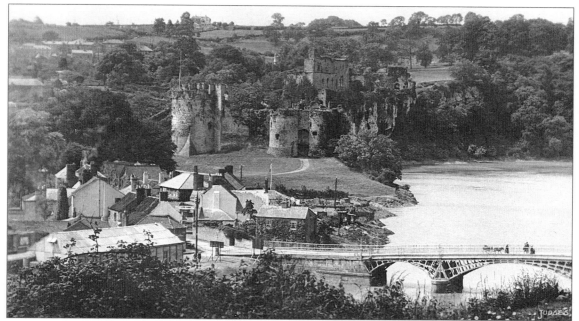

A closer look at the western approach to the old Chepstow road bridge – still, astonishingly, free of all traffic apart from a family out walking their dogs – or possibly donkeys. A section of the old town wall once ran down to this end of the bridge from the castle. Not until 1987 was the traffic congestion here eased when the bridge was superseded by a new steel and concrete one downriver and consequently demoted to minor road status. (*Judges' Ltd., Hastings*)

The Wye Valley Walk ends (and officially begins) in the castle car park beside the river, 136 miles from Plynlimon.

A last, timeless image from the upper reaches of this most romantic of rivers: man, coracle and the Wye in perfect harmony. (*Paget Prize Self Toning*)

Fitly to describe the Wye is an impossible task. Though its praises have been sung by generations of poets, it still has countless charms of which no word-picture has been drawn, and almost all that can be done in these plain, prosaic pages is to point out some of the beauty spots and how they may best be reached.

"Talk of the Wye as some old dream,
Call it the wild, the wizard stream,
The eye of genius may behold
A thousand beauties here untold."

(*A Pictorial and Descriptive Guide to the Wye Valley,*
Ward, Lock & Co. Ltd, 9th edition, revised)